LAW ENFORCEMENT TEST PREPARATION

How to Land a Law Enforcement Job

By: Lieutenant Tim C. Jones (Ret)

Vol. I

TABLE OF CONTENTS

Section 1: Introduction

My name is Tim Jones. I recently retired as a lieutenant after 20 years in law enforcement. Prior to my law enforcement career, I served in the U.S. Navy as a Deep Sea Diver (hoo-yah!). While serving as a diver, I was fortunate enough to work with some of finest and fittest people in the Navy.

During my law enforcement career, I was involved in a variety of capacities with the recruiting and testing of new hires. As I went up in rank, my area of control grew larger. Ultimately, I ran testing processes in their entirety - from the written test all of the way through background investigations. Adding to my test proctoring experience, while stationed at a US Navy Dive School, I assisted with testing processes for diver candidates.

So, why am I qualified to write a manual on how to prepare for a testing process? Well ladies and gentlemen, I have a vast amount of experience with testing processes and I have seen what works and what leaves you walking out the door with your head hanging. Not only have I been involved with many physical agility and written test processes, I have interviewed hundreds of candidates who want to be police officers and have observed the same mistakes over and over again.

I do not want you to make these mistakes. I want you to do the one thing that so many failed to do – PREPARE! Preparation equals confidence and confidence equals success. When candidates walk into a testing process with confidence and have a winning mindset, they are generally the ones that rise to the top and have a higher probability of getting hired.

This preparation manual is NOT a magic pill. There is no easy way to become prepared for a testing process. You will be required to put in some work. This preparation manual helps you focus your efforts into critical areas. You have taken the first step by purchasing this manual. So, let's cease with the pleasantries and get down to work!

Section 2: Failure is Not an Option!

War Story

When I first started my business, I would teach the contents of this manual to Criminal Justice majors. I met a young man at one of my seminars who was very enthusiastic and told me that he really wanted to be a police officer for the town in which I worked. I recognized him from my department's last testing process. Although he was a college senior, he was a bit out of shape. He had not made it through the hiring process in the aforementioned test.

After participating in my hiring seminar, the young man reevaluated his approach to the testing process. He told me in an email that he would follow my advice on preparing for the physical agility test, the written test and the oral board interview.

About a year later, I saw this same young man at my department's testing process. He was still very enthusiastic, as usual, but also much more physically fit. He did very well on his written test, which got him to the second phase of the process. He proceeded to destroy the physical agility test – he was an animal!

I had the opportunity to sit on his oral board interview. I could clearly see that his confidence was in a good place. He followed my advice to the tee. He even memorized the department's mission statement. He did an outstanding job and was at the top of the list. The funny thing is, he had also tested for another agency and had similar results. The other agency was able to move quicker and hired him first...our loss! This story, however, is not about my agency's loss; it is about this young man's success. He had created the ultimate scenario – he had more than one police department competing to hire him.

I had an opportunity to talk to this young man later on and I asked him how my tactics helped him. He said that the seminar he attended was invaluable and added that his preparation for the exams gave him strength, confidence and helped him create a personal mantra: FAILURE IS NOT AN OPTION!

Before you go any further in this manual, you need to make the following commitments to yourself:

1. I will put in the work
2. I will stay the course and not give up
3. I will have a **winning mindset**

Section 3: Applying for the Job

Law enforcement agencies are getting away from paper applications and moving to online measures. This is good because it saves you from having to fill out an application by hand and exposing your poor handwriting. It also saves on paper. However, there may still be some agencies that prefer paper applications. Let's talk about some do's and don'ts when filling one out.

First, if you can avoid filling it out by hand, do so. It may require some extra work on your part, but it will pay off in the end. There used to be these devices in the Paleolithic Era called typewriters. If you can find one, you can feed the application into the typewriter and fill out the responses that way. <u>Make some copies of the application first so you can figure out the spacing and alignment before feeding the actual application through</u>.

If you cannot find a typewriter, and you are tech savvy, you can scan the application and create a writable document. It is beyond my expertise, but I have seen applications come across my desk where someone took the time to do this. <u>It impressed me!</u>

If you are not able to use a typewriter or do not have the skills to create a writable scanned document, you will need to get a pen and start. Always use **black** ink. You should make copies of the application and practice filling it out first. PRINT LEGIBLY! If your handwriting is terrible, consider having someone with good handwriting fill it out for you.

Why does all of this matter, you ask? Because you only get one chance to make a good first impression. If your application looks like crap, then the reviewers will not think much of you. This is a good life skill for anything important you pursue. Put your best foot forward from the very beginning. I can tell you from experience that when my peers and I reviewed applications, we were always impressed with those who took the extra time to make their product look professional. Those applications stand out.

Second, when you pick up a paper application at a police department, do not go in looking like a hobo. You will see a recurring theme here – FIRST IMPRESSIONS MATTER. When you request an application, you may be speaking to someone who is involved with the hiring process, particularly at smaller agencies. The same goes when returning the application: look professional. You do not need to wear a suit, but at least look presentable and wear something besides shorts and a tee-shirt.

As stated earlier, many agencies use online applications. This saves you from having to drive to the agency to pick up an application (it is okay to fill it out in shorts and a tee-shirt, or even your underwear, whatever). My cautionary advice here is that you read the instructions carefully and make sure you complete the application fully and you attach EVERYTHING they request and in the fashion it is requested. If the agency wants a cover letter, resume and a list of references in one document, then that is how you do it. If they want them separately, then attach them separately. By not following the instructions as stated, you may be forfeiting an opportunity to test.

Make sure you adhere to deadlines. Late applications may not be accepted and worst of all, even if they are, you just became THAT GUY OR GAL. First impressions, right?

Many to most agencies will charge some sort of administrative fee to apply and test for law enforcement positions. This is standard procedure. The fees help offset the costs of the actual tests and the manpower needed to run the testing process. If the agency requests payment in the form of a bank check or money order, then you pay like that. Don't be the person that forgot to get the bank check and shows up with a personal check. When applying online, you may have to pay with a credit card.

First Impressions and Why They Matter

Do first impressions matter?

YES they do. They actually matter a great deal. The tone and/or direction of a conversation can be decided in a matter of seconds. Believe it or not, first impressions are mostly guided by our subconscious minds.

Our conscious brains can handle roughly 40 bits of information per second. Our unconscious minds can handle up to 11 million bits per second.

What does that mean? Since our conscious brains have a limited capacity for processing data, our brains have evolved to turn other functions over to the subconscious brain. When we see a stranger, our subconscious brains are immediately sizing the person up. Is he/she he friend or foe? Is he/she a potential mate? Can I trust this person?

Our subconscious minds also have a mirroring effect. If you come into contact with a friend that is upset, you may become upset. How many of you have ever noticed that emotions can be contagious?

Now, let's put this into the context of a job interview.

If you are extremely nervous, or maybe you are upset because of an argument with a friend, then when you walk into the interview room, you may start leaking your "negative" emotions to the interviewers. Do you want the interviewer to pick up negativity from you?

NO, you want to ooze confidence, happiness and optimism.
To project happiness, prior to walking into the interview, think of a happy time in your life. Focus on why it made you happy and how grateful you are to have experienced it.

We will get to a confidence building technique later in the discussion.

So, what's the end game here? You may only get one chance to make a good impression. The department personnel with which you interact will be sizing you up on a subconscious level – from their very first interaction with you. Project happiness and confidence from the onset, not anxiety, stress, anger, insecurity, or other negative emotions. You want people to mirror how you feel…especially those people that may potentially hire you.

To reinforce this idea, the **youtube.com link** below features a talk conducted by Olivia Fox Cabane on the topic of first impressions. I highly recommend watching it.

FIRST IMPRESSIONS:
https://www.youtube.com/watch?v=_zRZ5j2O07w

Resumes and Cover Letters

Most law enforcement agencies will require a resume and cover letter. Believe me, they are reviewed with a critical eye. Your resume will be read for relevant content, but it will also be combed over for mistakes. Why? Because a well-written and well-formatted resume tells the reader that you have taken the time to ensure it was done well. That translates to a person who pays attention to detail and takes pride in their work product.

Here are some quick tips on your resume and cover letter:

Cover Letter

- Use resume paper, in off-white (no blue or purple). Does not apply if emailing cover letter.
- Keep it to one (1) page
- Don't repeat your whole resume in your cover letter; find something new, but relevant, to speak about.
- Avoid stating who you are and what position you are applying for in the first paragraph – they know that.
- Explain your enthusiasm for the prospect of working for that agency and how your particular skills and qualifications will make you a good candidate.
- Here is a great link with cover letter examples: http://www.monster.com/career-advice/article/sample-cover-letter

Tim's Note: A failure that I have seen from many young candidates, with respects to resumes and cover letters, is that they don't highlight their college work experience (or pre-law enforcement experience) and how it can relate to law enforcement. For example, many people I have interviewed had worked in the restaurant industry. They felt that there was no correlation between being a waiter and being a police officer. This is simply not true. Police officers are servants and are in essence "waiting" on a customer (citizen) who is in need. Also, waiters and waitresses may deal with irate customers and learn how to deescalate tension to create a positive outcome, just like law enforcement officers. Are you picking up what I'm putting down? Don't undersell yourself because you worked minimum wage jobs in high school or college.

Resume

- Use resume paper, in off-white (no blue or purple). Does not apply if emailing resume.
- Do not use fancy borders and colorful stripes. Use the KISS principal – Keep It Super Simple.
- Use black ink only
- Keep it to two (2) pages.
- Use a professional font, such as Times New Roman
- Under each job you've held, identify your duties (briefly) and also any accomplishments (promotions, awards, etc.)
- Make sure you highlight skills that will be beneficial in a law enforcement job such as communication, conflict resolution, working in teams, writing, working in a structured environment, wearing a uniform, adhering to policies and procedures, observing chain of command, etc.
- If you are required to print your resume, make sure the ink is clear and looks good (no fades or stripes due to low ink).

War Story

My department was holding interviews for a patrol officer position. Three of us were reviewing resumes before the candidates came in. I was handed a resume by a sergeant on the board with the comment, "You're gonna love this one, LT."

Have you ever seen a printed document that came from a printer that was pretty much out of ink or toner? That is what this person submitted. It was so bad, I could not read most of the resume. To make matters worse, the candidate was a former police officer.

Needless to say, I was not impressed. I went downstairs and met privately with this individual. I explained that the resume was not acceptable and being a former law enforcement officer (LEO), she should have known better. After an attempt at an excuse, I told her that she was all done.

Now before you think me a complete A**hole, think about my perspective. The best LEO's are the ones that pay attention to detail. They are the ones that take pride in their work and always deliver a professional product. The above described young lady did not take the time to hand in a professional product. What kind of police officer would she be? Her work-product (resume) did not give me the impression that she would take pride in her work.

Tim's Note: If you had a moment of youthful indiscretion and created a humorous email address, such as studmuffin@gmail, or twerk4U@gmail, DO NOT use it on your resume and cover letter. Take the time to obtain a more "conservative" email address.

Here is a resume example. This format has worked for me.
Feel free to use the same format for your resume.

Timothy C. Jones
22 Fake Drive
Faketown, NJ
Email.com   phone number

Qualifications

Having worked in law enforcement for 20 years, I recently retired with the rank of
Lieutenant. I have supervisory experience as a Patrol Sergeant, Detective/Sergeant and
Lieutenant. I served as the department's Grant Coordinator and was the administrative
supervisor of the Detective Bureau and TAR Team. I have extensive history with criminal
investigations, internal investigations, administrative reviews, background investigations,
budgetary processes and various research projects and committees. I also have experience
with teaching a variety of law enforcement topics.

Employment History

2014–present   **Owner, Granite State Police Career Counseling, LLC**

- Author of "Leadership Development" course for First-Line Supervisors
- Author of "Report Writing 101" course for Law Enforcement
- Author of "Police Test Preparation" course & study guide
- Organize and coordinate classes with Law Enforcement Agencies throughout New England

2010-2016   **Lieutenant, Londonderry Police Department**

- Shift Commander for various shifts – Patrol and Airport
- Created and reviewed department and public policy
- Conducted internal investigations and administrative reviews
- Administrative head of the Detective Bureau
- Administrative head of the Traffic Accident Reconstruction Team
- Managed the department's Services Division

2005-2010   **Patrol Sergeant, Londonderry Police Department**

- First-line supervisor for police patrol functions

- First-line supervisor for law enforcement operations at the Manchester/Boston Regional Airport
- Provided training and evaluations for patrol and airport police personnel

2006-2007   Detective Sergeant, Londonderry Police Department

- Directly supervised four detectives
- Conducted and coordinated training for detectives
- Coordinated all hiring procedures for the department, including testing, background investigations and admission to the NH Police Academy

2002-2005   Detective, Londonderry Police Department

- Investigated criminal cases, maintained department pawn records and sex offender registrations
- Processed crime scenes for forensic evidence
- Background investigations for department and town personnel

1996-2002   Patrolman, Londonderry Police Department

- Performed all required duties of a patrolman
- Mountain Bike patrol during the summer
- Served on the Southern New Hampshire Special Operations Unit for six years as an operator and sniper (SWAT)

Education and Relevant Professional Development

2003 – 2009   **University of Phoenix,** BS – Criminal Justice Administration; GPA 3.79
1995 – 1996   **New Hampshire Technical Institute,** AS – Criminal Justice; GPA 3.96
2011 – 2011   Primex Human Resource Academy
2011 – 2011   Internal Investigations Class at PSTC (Chuck Hemp)
2007 – 2007   Massachusetts Police Leadership Institute, Police Leadership Training
2015 – 2015   FBI LEEDA Command Leadership Course
1996 – 1996   New Hampshire Police Academy

Notice that this resume is organized, easy to follow and *conservative*.

There are hundreds of examples of resumes on the internet. All that matters is that you stay away from fancy fonts and colors. Remember your audience. Keep it simple, easy to follow and conservative.

Section 4: PREPARING FOR THE WRITTEN TEST

A question that I would often get at my seminars is, how does one prepare for a test when one does not know what will be on the test? That is a very good question. In my home state of New Hampshire, there is no state standard for written tests. That means it's up to each agency to procure and administer their own test. This practice is not uncommon. Some agencies will purchase tests from reputable testing companies, such as IPMA-HR or IOS Solutions. Some agencies create their own test. I am also seeing trends where certain entities, such as a college, will sponsor regional tests. Many states rely on a civil service type exam (state-wide regional test). Below are a few law enforcement testing norms:

The majority of LE tests are multiple choice
They are designed to measure basic abilities and skill sets
Most are timed, which adds an element of stress
They will be strictly proctored

Law enforcement agencies have a variety of testing resources available. But, there is some good news. All of these tests typically follow a pattern of related criteria.

Observe and Recall

As a LE officer, you will be expected to observe people, vehicles or other items and then recall them at a later time. A LE exam may test your ability to just that.

This part of the exam is typically executed by having you read a series of pages that contain descriptors of people, actions and possibly images. You will be given a certain amount of time to look over the pages and then those pages will be collected. You will then be asked a series of questions about your observations. This is a skill you can practice at home. Look at a magazine picture for two minutes. Then have a friend take it from you and ask you specific questions, testing your recall for details.

Judgment, Deduction & Problem Solving Abilities

LE officers are often confronted with situations where they must use judgment and reasoning in order to make a decision or solve a problem. Examples include deciding whether to arrest someone, deciding what information is more reliable and deciding what tactics to employ to gain compliance with unwilling or excited people. Tests may involve written scenarios that candidates read, followed by a series of problem solving questions.

Basic Math and Grammar Knowledge

Math – You may see some basic math on a LE test. The problems are not at a quantum physics level. The math will be basic and may be in the form of word problems. If math is not your best area, you can brush up on some basics here: http://www.basic-mathematics.com/

Here is a link to my webpage where you can purchase a study guide specifically for math questions on a police exam:

GS-PCC.com Recommended Study Guides:
https://www.gs-pcc.com/recommended-books---study-guides.html

Grammar – It is very common for LE tests to assess you on certain grammar, vocabulary and reading comprehension skills. You may be required to read a series of paragraphs and then answer questions about the content. You may be asked language arts questions regarding punctuation and spelling. These tests are not looking for Master's Degree level language arts professionals; rather, the test is evaluating basic level grammar skills. Why? Because most law enforcement professionals are required to write reports, emails or memorandums. It is very important that you have a solid grasp on how to perform basic writing tasks.

We will discuss methods to help improve reading comprehension later, but if you need to brush up on your grammar and vocabulary skills, I recommend these sites:

http://grammar.yourdictionary.com/spelling-and-word-lists/misspelled.html

http://www.skillsyouneed.com/write/grammar2.html

Below is a breakdown by subtest of the police officer test offered by IPMA-HR, a very reputable testing company. As you can see, it follows the criteria pattern I mentioned earlier.

Subtests	Number of Test Items Per Subtest
Ability to Learn and Apply Police Information (TIP)	25
Ability to Observe and Remember Details (TIP)/(VID)	12
Verbal Ability*	23
Ability to Follow Directions	20
Ability to Problem Solve and Use Logic & Ability to Use Situational Judgment	The 100 series combines Situational Judgment & Problem Solving. There are 20 items on each test.
Total	100

Written Test Preparation – The Easy Way

After you apply to a LE agency, you should take the time to find out which testing company they use for their written exam. If the agency will not tell you or you cannot find it via a search on the internet, no worries. We will discuss other study methods later on. But, if you do know which testing company is being used, it would be worth your while to obtain the respective company's study guide, if they offer one.

Here are various law enforcement testing companies that provide written exams for LE agencies in the US. Below each company is a link to their respective study guide. Some are free and some you have to pay for…..sorry.

IPMA-HR – Police Entry-Level Exam

http://ipma-hr.org/assessment/study/poelsg2nd

EB Jacobs – Police Entry-Level Exam

GS-PCC.com Recommended Books

Fire & Police Selection, Inc. - Police Entry Level Exam

http://www.fpsi.com/online-practice-test-disclaimer/

McCann Associates – Police Entry Level Exam

McCanntesting.com

Morris & McDaniel – Police Entry Level Exam

http://morrisandmcdaniel.com/pages/home_police.htm

Standard & Associates – Police Entry-Level Exam

https://www.applytoserve.com/Study/

*(**Note:** The links provided above are for police tests. Some of these companies do provide tests for corrections officers and dispatchers)*

In my research, I found an online company, www.jobtestprep.com, that is a clearing house for LE test preparation, listing links to civil service exams and various police test vendors (listed individually above). There is a fee for their services, but they seem to simplify the process by helping you find the appropriate testing company for your state or area. This company also assists you with preparing for that particular exam. I did not subscribe, but from what I can tell from their claims, if I were preparing for a written test, I would use them. Below is a link to their site:

Job Test Prep – Setting Standards in Assessment Test Prep.

https://www.jobtestprep.com/police-exam-preparation

Civil Service Exams

Civil service exams are the first stage of entry into a civil service job. The exam may be written, or written followed by other exams, such as an oral exam or a scenario-based exam. Civil service exams typically rank the participants by score. The better you do, the higher you are on the list.

Some states require law enforcement agencies to make selections based on the civil service exam. There are also civil service exams for federal LE jobs. There are some pros and cons to this system. If the exam is state mandated, then you will be competing with a lot of people. The flip side to that is that every LE agency will be pulling from that list. Most civil service exams will allow you to select where you would like to work. Maybe you want to stay in a certain region of your state; thus, moving 200 miles away for a job may not be a good option for you.

Although I do not have direct experience with civil service exams, my research has found that there are many study guides available. Given the amount of competition, I highly recommend investing in one of these guides. If you are looking to get into law enforcement in your state, be sure to check on whether the agency you want to work for participates in the civil service exam process. If so, do the research and find a study guide for that particular exam.

Written Test Preparation – The Not As Easy Way

But Tim, what if I do not know which written test is being used by the LE agency I applied for?

That is a good question. There are ways to prepare for taking a LE written test without using specific study guides. It just takes a little more effort.

As I stated earlier, most LE written tests follow a certain content pattern – observe & recall, reading comprehension, reasoning, grammar and possibly some math. Let's look at some approaches to each of these areas that can help you prepare:

Observe & Recall – These tests will have you read reports and/or view images of various people and items. After the reference material is collected, you will be asked questions on what you read and saw. You need to start training your mind to do just that – see things and then recall them. If you practice it, you will get better at it.

Practice:

Read this example of a police report and then try to answer all of the questions **without** going back to find the answers.

Officer Doe's police report:

On June 19, 2013, at 12:10 PM, I was dispatched to 26 Fake Rd. for a theft complaint. Upon arrival, I met with the victim, Steven Nichols DOB 1/1/75. Nichols stated that on the previous night, he went to the Sand Shaker Lounge at 7:00 PM and had some drinks. While doing so, he met two female subjects. He identified the females as RACHEL MONTGOMERY and SUSAN EMMONS.

Nichols stated that he, Montgomery and Emmons had a few drinks together and made the decision to go to his house in order to have a few more beers and watch a movie. Nichols reported that he drove his car and the two females followed him in their car. Nichols stated that the car was operated by Emmons and it was a blue, Dodge minivan. He was not sure of the year model. He stated that the van had a New Hampshire vanity plate - SUGAR.

Nichols stated that the three arrived at his home around 10:30 PM. He said that they consumed a six-pack of beer that he had in his refrigerator. Nichols reported that he was pretty intoxicated and many of the details are not clear. He stated that at one point, he went to the bathroom; he was not sure of the exact time. Upon returning to the living room area, Montgomery and Emmons were gone.

I asked Nichols if he had angered the women. He stated that he did not think so. I asked him what happened after that. Nichols said that he did not have the females' cell phone numbers, so he could not call them. He reported that he went to bed soon after they left.

Nichols said that at around 10:00 AM the next morning, he woke up and was looking for his cell phone. He stated that he could not find it. This led Nichols to also look for his wallet. He stated that his cell phone and wallet were missing and he is sure that he had them when he, Montgomery and Emmons arrived at his house.

- What lounge did Nichols go to?
- What time did he arrive?
- What was Montgomery's first name?
- What type of car did Emmons drive?
- What was the license plate?

- What time did the three arrive at Nichols's home?
- What was Nichols missing?

Preparation Tips

Tip 1 – Find a magazine article that has some images with it. Read the article and put it down. Recall, in order, the main points of the article. Try to remember details, such as names or places. Also, try to recall details about the images. After you have recalled as much as possible, read it again and repeat the process. Do you see where I'm going here? You are teaching your mind how to observe and then recall. Do this often with varying articles.

Tip 2 – Read non-fiction material (newspaper or trade magazine) about something you are not familiar with. After reading it, recall the article in your head and more importantly, focus on the details. Why read something I'm not familiar with? Because if you read material you know, your recall and comprehension will not truly be tested – you know the material. If it is unknown to you, your mind will have to work harder to comprehend and recall it.

Below is a link from wikihow.com on how to improve reading comprehension:

http://www.wikihow.com/Improve-Your-Reading-Comprehension

Tip 3 – If you are not good with grammar, read up on the basics. LE tests are not looking to see if you know what a dangling participle is. They are testing your knowledge on basic grammar. Do you know how to properly use a comma? There are numerous free websites that review basic grammar rules. My company teaches a report writing class and we recommend Barron's Painless Grammar by Rebecca Elliott Ph.D.

Tip 4 – This is one of the most important tips. Although we are training our minds to observe and recall and understand grammar rules, we also need to train our minds to take a test. I have had SO many people tell me that they are just not good test takers. The first thing that I tell them is that if they keep telling themselves that, then it will certainly be true...**so stop saying it!** The next thing I tell them is that they may have a fear or anxiety when it comes to tests. So how do we fix that? We take A LOT of tests!

There are many law enforcement test preparation books available on Amazon or at Barnes & Nobles that are relatively inexpensive (see links below). All of them contain practice tests. Part of your preparation strategy should include taking practice tests. Remember that we are in the category of not knowing which written test we are going to take; therefore, we are preparing our minds to be comfortable with taking a test.

The LE test preparation books mentioned below are NOT test specific. In other words, if you know that an agency you applied to is using a test from IPMA-HR, an Arco LE exam study guide will not necessarily have released questions from that test. The generic LE test study guides (for example, Arco) get their material from nationwide surveys and research. In other words, they use trends. The questions on the generic guide tests may or may not help you with actual content. *But by taking these tests, you are getting into test taking mode*. You will become comfortable with reading a question and using reasoning to pick A, B, C or D.

If you purchase one or two of these generic books, make copies of the answer sheets. Then, take tests twice per week. Don't worry about retaking the same tests. I recommend reviewing the answers and making corrections to the ones you got wrong. Again, there may be some questions on the generic test that are very similar to the questions you see on the real exam.

Here are some good generic LE study guides:

Police Officer Exam for Dummies
Barron's Police Officer Exam, 9th Edition
Learning Express – Corrections Officer Exam
Corrections Officer Exam Study Guide
Public Safety Dispatcher/911 Operator
Master the Special Agent Exam
Deputy Sheriff – by Passbook

*All of these can be found at: https://www.gs-pcc.com/
recommended-books---study-guides.html*

More Test Taking Tips

- Make sure you get plenty of sleep the night before the test
- Make sure you arrive well nourished. Don't change your breakfast routine. You do not need stomach issues during the test.
- Arrive early. Any anxiety or stress about being late will interfere with your ability to concentrate on the test. ALSO, if you arrive late, you may not be allowed to take the test.
- Make sure you know how to get to the testing site. Don't wait until the day of to figure out where the test is being held.
- Think positive. A positive attitude will help create a positive outcome.
- Ensure you follow the directions that are given. Do not improvise. If you do something that annoys the test proctors, you just became "that guy or gal."
- If you are not sure about the instructions given, ask for clarification…it's okay to ask.

- Read each question carefully and ensure that your question number matches the answer sheet number. It would suck to get questions wrong because you were putting your answers on the wrong line of the answer sheet.
- If you do not know the answer to a question, use the process of elimination to narrow down your choices. Eliminate the selections that are clearly wrong and try to deduct an answer from there.

Extra Tips:

- Bring your state ID in with you. You may have to prove who you are.
- Bring two, number two pencils. Most agencies will provide you with a pencil, but you never know.
- Leave your cell phone in your car!!! You will not need it.
- Be respectful and give it your all.

Section 5: PREPARING FOR THE PHYSICAL AGILITY TEST

Why would you be required to take a physical agility test in order to be hired as a law enforcement officer? The answer is, why would you not? Law enforcement work can be physically demanding and stressful. Also, a LE agency wants to make sure that first, you can make it through an academy, and second, you can handle incidents where physical agility is needed.

So how do we prepare for this test? This my friends is the easy part. It is easy because you will likely know the answers before the test. When you apply, if there is a physical agility test, the agency should provide you with the minimum standards. You will know what is expected of you in advance – YAY!

What to expect

The physical agility test will vary from state to state and agency to agency. Many follow Cooper Aerobics Institute standards. What are Cooper Standards? Basically, Cooper takes a set of physical exercises, such as push-ups or a run, and categorizes a percentile range based on age and gender. For example, a 22 year old male may be expected to do a certain number of push-ups in order to fall into a percentile group. I know this may be a little confusing. Just understand that what you are expected to do on a physical agility test may vary based on your age and gender.

If you apply for a law enforcement job and there is a physical agility test and the agency does not provide you with the qualification standards, you MUST do some research and find out. You may need to call the agency and get an answer. The standards may be listed on the agency's website. It is important that you know so you know what to prepare for.

Here is a question for you: if people know in advance what the physical agility standards are, then why do so many applicants fail? This one boggles my mind.

War Story

My agency was conducting a testing process for a patrol officer position. As is our procedure, we put a copy of the physical agility standards in every application. There was a young lady who was taking the physical agility test who had not prepared. She was overweight and was not at all ready for the run portion of the test.

Within three laps (out of six), she collapsed. An ambulance was summoned. While tending to her, she stated that she was asthmatic and needed her inhaler. It was in her car, not with her. Also, while she was lying on the ground, her cigarettes and lighter fell out of her pocket. So, she felt that it was important to bring her butts with her, but not her inhaler....

How to Prepare

The first step is knowing what will be expected of you. Once you have that, you can start your Rocky Balboa workout routine.

The biggest mistake that many candidates make is that they assume they are fit enough for the test. They don't run themselves through a test to see if they can pass everything. It has been my experience that men and women who are good at lifting weights and are muscular and very strong will sometimes assume that they can run 1.5 miles with no problem. Or, a very good runner may assume that he or she can bench press their body weight. Well, guess what, most of the failures that I have witnessed fall into these aforementioned groups.

So what is your point Tim? My point is, don't assume – PREPARE! Let's say that you have to perform the following exercises at a LE entry exam:

Bench Press Body Weight
Push-ups
Sit-ups
300 Yard Sprint
1.5 mile run

You should be working on:

Bench Press
Push-ups
Sit-ups

Sprints
The 1.5 mile run

Do I need to explain it any further? Now I know that many of you are gym rats or worship at the alter of Crossfit, but I'm telling you that in order to do very well on your physical agility test, focus on the exercises that you need to do. You can still work out in other ways, but just put an emphasis on the test exercises until the day of the test.

This segues into my next point. It **MUST** be your mission to not just pass your physical agility test, but to knock it out of the park. If you are expected to do 35 push-ups, you should knock out 65.

But why, Tim? Remember I told you about first impressions and how they are important? The physical agility test is a good way to show the agency that you don't settle for the minimums. Also, the entire law enforcement field is macho-istic. LE officers tend to be athletic (though certainly not all of them) and they will chatter to each other about a person's physical accomplishments during the physical agility test – I've observed this many times.

My point here is that you should not shoot for the minimum scores. Push yourself when you workout so that you go above and beyond at the actual test.

Workout Recommendations

DISCLAIMER – I am not a personal trainer nor am I a doctor. The recommendations listed below are just that – **recommendations**. It is advised that you consult with your physician before starting a new workout regimen. ALWAYS USE CAUTION WHEN WORKING OUT!

- Start with a full test to establish a baseline. Record your results.
- Incorporate the exercises on the test into your normal workout. If you don't workout, it's time to start. Focus on the test exercises.
- When you work on the exercises, push yourself to max each time
- When you work on the run, add an additional half-mile so that your endurance is heightened. For example, if you have to run 1.5 miles, when you train, run 2 miles. If there is a sprint portion, say 300 yards, practice sprinting 350 yards.
- Consider interval training for your runs. Here is a link from active.com – Interval Training - *http://www.active.com/ running/articles/3-interval-training-plans-to-build-fitness-fast*
- When you train, do the exercises in different orders. Don't get locked into a certain order and then get out of whack if you have to conduct the test in a different order on test day.
- Do not over-train and do not push yourself to injury. Keep it steady and strive to make improvements each time you self-test.

Your goal should be to exceed the minimum standards by as much as you possibly can.

Note: During my research, I have found that some LE agencies only want the candidates to do the minimum number of exercises. This is mostly due to time management. So, if you are told to do 35 push-ups and stop, then that is what you do. Do not keep going if you are told to stop. If you do, you just became THAT GUY OR GAL!

Do not go into a testing process with the mindset that you will be asked to do the minimums. Always be prepared to max out.

THE DAY OF THE TEST

- Make sure you get plenty of rest the day and night before
- Don't change your normal eating and hydration routine - in other words, don't eat or drink something you've never had before - especially energy drinks.
- Make sure you hydrate, starting the day before
- How and when the test is administered, and in what order, is up to the department. Some will conduct the PT test first, followed by the written, and some will conduct it the other way around. Some departments may conduct the written on one day and conduct the PT on a different day.
- What does that mean to you? Be flexible. Don't get worked up about the test order. It's okay to take a written test while you are sweaty.
- The order of the exercises may vary. Most departments will save the run for last. Make sure you follow directions closely.

Note: Make sure that when you train, you are doing the exercises correctly. If the standard for sit-ups is to interlace your hands behind your head, then practice that way. If you practice with your hands cupped behind your ears, then on the day of the test, your number of sit-ups will be reduced due to not executing them properly. The same goes for push-ups. Ensure that you have a straight back and that you touch the floor with your chest and that your arms are almost fully extended while up.

Below are some links that provide instruction on how to properly do push-ups and sit-ups:

Push-ups - https://www.youtube.com/watch?v=IODxDxX7oi4

Sit-ups - https://www.youtube.com/watch?v=s_4V6_dpObI

*note the hand position in the video. Practice sit-ups with your hands in these positions:

o Hands interlaced behind head
o Hands behind head but not interlaced
o Hands cupped behind ears
o Hands crossing, touch each shoulder

TEST DAY DO'S AND DON'TS

Do's
- Be respectful to all staff running the PT test, in many cases they are volunteering their time
- Seek clarification if you do not understand an exercise or instructions
- Dress appropriately - bring or wear proper attire for a PT test
- Give it your all - Do not do just the minimums if you have more in you (unless you are specifically asked to stop!)

Don'ts
- Don't try to engage the staff with idle conversation. Your intentions may be good, but they may see it as kissing up.
- Don't show off - no one-handed push-ups or displays of karate or acrobatic skills - I have seen it and it did not go well!
- Don't complain about the testing process. The quickest way to find your file in a trashcan is to criticize someone's hard

work. Testing processes are not easy to run. If it is not going the way you like it, either adapt and move on, or leave.

Now that you know what to do, get off of your ass and prepare!

Section 6: PREPARING FOR THE ORAL BOARD INTERVIEW

THE NEXT PHASE

Congratulations, you passed your written and PT test. You are on your way to the next phase of the hiring process. Typically, the next step in the hiring process is the oral board interview. Every department is different as to when oral boards are offered and how they are run. Some oral boards can be very lengthy and some are brief. Some are quite adversarial and some are adversarial "lite." They are all designed to see how you handle yourself under pressure and how well you express and explain your thought processes.

Preparing For Your Interview

Attire:

- **Men** - Wear a conservative suit, preferably black, gray or dark blue, with a conservative shirt and conservative tie. You may be the next Men's Health or GQ model, but if you show up wearing fashion colors, you suddenly became **"that guy."**
- Wear a suit that fits. Resist the temptation to borrow your friend's suit that is two sizes too small or too big. Invest in a new, properly fitted suit.
- Do NOT wear wrinkled clothes. If you cannot take the time to iron your shirt, a LE agency does not want you!

- Wear proper dress shoes. If you show up wearing sneakers with your suit because it is an expression of your personality, you will probably be asked to leave.

VS

- **Women** - With respect to attire, you have more options than men; however, your goal should be a conservative appearance as well.
- It does not matter if your hair is up or down, just ensure that it is well groomed and professional.
- Avoid loud colors and stick with simple, understated jewelry.

OR

Grooming

- I won't tell you that you have get your hair buzzed or get rid of your beard, but understand that if you want to work in law enforcement, it is good to look the part. Typically, facial hair is not in keeping with a LE's grooming policy.
- Men should not wear earrings.
- Men should not wear anything on their wrists except a watch.
- If you have unnatural colors in your hair (e.g. pink, blue, purple, etc), you should have it corrected before your oral board interview (potentially even before your written & PT - think: **good first impressions)**
- Women's make-up should be conservative.
- **No perfume or cologne!** - no one wants to be starved for oxygen during the interview - been there, done that!
- What's the bottom line here? Don't give the board something to focus on other than what you have to say.

Walking Into the Room

- Once again, we are on to **first impressions.**
- The board wants to see confidence.....not arrogance.
- Stand up straight with your shoulders and chin up (not too far up).
- You will more than likely be escorted in. Typically there will be a table in the room where board members will sit opposite to you.
- You should walk to the first board member, look him/her in the eye and put your hand out for a handshake. Once you shake hands, introduce yourself - confidently: "Hello Sir/ Ma'am, John Candidate."

- Your handshake grip should match the grip of the hand you are shaking – Don't have a dead fish handshake or try to break someone's hand.

Taking A Seat

There will be a seat directly across from the board members. Do not sit down until you are asked to do so. Some boards will not care if you sit down without being instructed to do so; however, there are some that do. You will not know what kind of board it is; thus, assume it is a board that wants you to wait and be asked to sit.

Posture

If the chair is near the table, do not lean on the table. Sit upright with your hands in your lap. If you cross your legs and/or arms, the board may interpret the posture as "protected" and may not feel confident with your answers. Remember, these are law enforcement professionals and many know how to read body language.

*O = Good   **X = Bad**

Tim's Note: I don't recommend bringing anything to the interview. The only thing that would be acceptable, if I were interviewing you, is a small folder with extra resumes in it. Do not bring water bottles or recreational books. If possible, leave your coat in your car. You don't want to be looking for a place to hang your coat while the board waits. The less you bring with you, the less you have to worry about.

Now - SMILE, BREATHE and maintain eye contact!

Speaking during the interview:

- You do not have to push your volume level while answering questions. In other words, do not yell.
- Speak at your normal cadence and at your normal conversational volume...not your barroom conversational volume.
- Do not mumble. If you are nervous, take a deep breath and speak clearly.
- It is okay to incorporate your hands while you speak...if that is how you normally communicate.

What kind of questions will you be asked?

There are basically 4 categories:
1. Introductory (ice breakers)
2. Scenario Based (ethical)
3. Probing or Data Questions
4. Personal Questions

Introductory Questions

These questions are "icebreakers" or "getting to know you" questions. A very common introductory question is: "Tell us about yourself."

THIS IS ONE OF THE MOST IMPORTANT QUESTIONS
FOR YOU TO GET RIGHT!

Why, you ask? Because this is where you get the opportunity to sell yourself. It is your time to shine. So what should you say?

Here are the main areas that you may choose to tell the board about:

- Family
  Relationship status
  Whether you have children
  Siblings
- Where you grew up
- If you went to college, talk about your major, your activities while in college (clubs, sports, organizations, etc), and your GPA
- If you currently have a job, explain where you work and what you do. Think about how this job may correlate to a law enforcement job. For example, if you work in retail, emphasize how you work with people and assist them or work out complaints that they may have
- Military experience - explain what you did
- **IMPORTANT** - describe your hobbies and interests.
  It is good for a board to know that you have outlets and have life outside of work

While talking, maintain eye contact with each board member while explaining your answers. Don't fixate on just the individual that asked the question.

<u>DO NOT BE MONOTONE</u> - BUELLER, BUELLER...

Look at it from their perspective; the board has been listening to candidates all day, maybe even all week. If you sound like Ben Stein, you are going to bore them and their focus will drift. Speak confidently, with your head up and your eyes on the board members. Speak with enthusiasm. Your excitement may just shake them out of a stupor.

Data Questions

If you want to work for a certain law enforcement agency, you damn well better do your homework about the agency and the area that they cover. For example, if you want to work for the Faketown Police Department, or the Fakestate Department of Corrections, then you need to know details about the agency and the area they serve.

Details to know about an agency:

- The size of the agency (number of sworn and non-sworn employees)
- The name of the top boss (Chief, Warden, Colonel, etc.)
- How the department is structured (divisions, departments, bureaus, etc.)
- Some of the crime statistics
- A few points from the department's mission statement (you don't have to memorize it, but it is impressive when people do) – webpage
- The square mileage of the town and the population
- Other demographics
- Who the town manager/administrator/mayor is

Resources for finding this material:
- Internet (department and town/city websites)
- 2010 census data
- Town/city report

DO NOT BE THE GUY OR GAL THAT THE BOARD HAS TO DRAG INFORMATION FROM!!

If you are a Criminal Justice student/graduate, you had better study up on the Constitutional Amendments that pertain to LE:

- 4th Amendment
- 5th Amendment
- 6th Amendment
- 8th Amendment

Scenario Based Questions

Board members will put you in a scenario where you are an employee of their agency. Believe me, the scenario will have "complications." They are not going to serve you softballs all day. You will not be required to know specific information, such as, whether the law allows for an arrest, or other procedural tactics. The board is looking at your decision-making ability.

You can ask for clarification on a question, or you may ask a procedural question. For example, if you are given a scenario where you are asked if you would arrest someone or not, and you are not sure if you can "legally" arrest the person, it is okay to ask if you can legally arrest or not. The question is more than likely examining your discretionary decision making skills - would you arrest and why or why not?

IMPORTANT: DO NOT TELL THE BOARD WHAT YOU THINK THEY WANT TO HEAR!!! ANSWER QUESTIONS TRUTHFULLY AND THOUGHTFULLY!

The board will be able to tell if you are trying to please them with your answer rather than answering how you truly feel.

You will more than likely have to back up your answers. Simply explain your thought process and how you came to that particular conclusion. The board will probably try to get you to change your answer. If a board member is simply asking you, "Are sure that is what you would do?" then stick to your answer - if you are certain about it. *If the board presents different facts, or changes the scenario slightly, your answer may change, given the circumstances. This is okay.*

Black & White Answers:

When I get candidates that are very black and white with their discretionary questions, I will often take them down the road of whom they would give a ticket. It may start with a good friend and ultimately end with their mother. This is an age-old question, but it helps the board decide on whether the candidate is saying what they truly feel, or just saying what they think the board wants to hear.

Would you give your mother a ticket? Of course you would NOT!

Scenario-based Ethical Questions

Many questions on law enforcement oral boards will put you in some sort of ethical dilemma. Many of the questions will start small and build their way up. The questions are looking to see what your threshold is for taking some sort of "official" action.

Here is a common police officer question - you and another officer are at a business alarm. While checking the interior, the other officer takes something small (e.g., candy bar, soda, lottery ticket, etc). What would you do?

Many candidates want to invoke the "blue line" standard and say that they would talk to the officer later, but would do nothing else.

What is wrong with that answer?

What does it open you up to?

If your answer was that you would do nothing or tell the officer to not do it again, you probably answered incorrectly.

Let's break it down. You are a law enforcement officer and you just witnessed a theft. If it were anyone else, you would arrest them. The officer with you just committed a crime. That is not acceptable and I don't feel that it should be tolerated.

BUT, I get the brother/sisterhood and I am not suggesting that you should arrest the officer with you. So, then, what is the best answer?

The answer that always worked best for me and for the other officers joining me on the board was when a candidate *told the thieving officer that he would give him until the end of the shift to tell the supervisor what he did, or he would tell the supervisor.* This is a good answer because it now places the burden on the thieving officer to make it right. You will need to back up the answer. You can always say that you are giving the thieving officer an opportunity to make it right.

To beat this dead horse some more, if you tolerate the officer taking something trivial, then chances are, there will be follow-up questions where the stakes are raised.

The board will keep asking you "what if" questions – what if he steals a six-pack of soda, what if he steals a bag of groceries? They are looking to see where your threshold is for where you will do something.

If you had done something in the beginning, they would not take you down this line of questioning.

REMEMBER, with ethics based questions, always do the right thing. **Always take the path of honor**.

<u>Tim's definition of honor</u>: Do the right thing, even when it SUCKS to do so!

PERSONAL QUESTIONS

These questions are to clarify to the board exactly who you are. Be honest with these questions and be prepared to "wow" them. A popular personal question is, "Tell us about some strengths and some weaknesses." Usually discussing two to three of each is sufficient.

You should be prepared for this one. The strengths are easy to talk about. Who doesn't love bragging about themselves? The weaknesses on the other hand, can be more difficult. Be prepared with ACTUAL weaknesses. No one likes to hear about how you are a perfectionist to a fault. This is the old "take something negative and flip it around with a positive spin" trick. I want to know who you are. We all have weaknesses, let's hear them.

You can follow up with how you deal with your weaknesses. For example, people have varying degrees of procrastination. People who tend to procrastinate have different ways in which they deal with those tendencies. Describe how you recognize your weaknesses and compensate for them. Maybe you are a person that doesn't take criticism very well. Tell this to the board and be prepared to discuss how you plan on dealing with it, as you will likely face criticism in the first few years of being a police officer.

Other examples of personal questions:
- Tell us about something that you've done that you are not proud of.
- Tell us why you want to be a police officer.
- What have you done to prepare yourself for this position?
- What characteristics do you feel are important for being a police officer or corrections officer, dispatcher, etc?

IMPORTANT NOTE - Some questions may have several sections or parts. Listen carefully to each part and answer them in the order that they were presented. For example: What are the characteristics of a police officer; why are they important and do you possess these characteristics?

Remember, clarification is okay – just ask.

PREPARATION

So, how do we prepare for an adversarial interview when we have never been through one before? Let me tell you!

First, below is a list of possible oral board questions. Read these questions and think about how you would answer them. When you read a question, categorize it – is it an icebreaker, a personal question, a scenario question or a data question?

Once you are comfortable on how you would answer it, alter the question a little and think about your answer. Now you are thinking and getting your mind ready for these types of questions.

POSSIBLE ORAL BOARD QUESTIONS

- Tell us about yourself.

- What have you done to prepare for this interview?

- What can you tell us about the town/city?

- What can you tell us about the department/jail/prison/etc?

- Is there something in your life that you are not proud of doing? What?

- Tell us some of your strengths and weaknesses.

- Why do you want to be a LEO? When did you decide on this career?

- What is the job of a LEO? Are you qualified?

- What have you done to prepare for this position?

- What are you bringing to the job?

- Why do you want to work for this city or agency?

- What do you like to do? What are your hobbies?

- What would your current or past employer say about you?

- What are the attributes of a LEO? What is the most important one to you?

- Are you on any other hiring lists? What would you do if another agency called you?

- When can you start if we offered you the job?

- How far do you want to go in the service? Where do you see yourself in 5, 10, 15 years?

- What are the best traits of a LEO? Which one is the most important to you?

- Have you ever been in an emergency situation? Tell us what you did?

- What word(s) would best describe you in a positive way? A negative way?

- How do you handle conflict?

- Why would we select you over the other candidates?

Scenario Questions (Ethics)

- You are put in a scenario where you are off duty and drugs are being used

- You are put in a scenario where another police officer commits an illegal act

More Preparation

Now the final touches. Divide the questions into groups of 5. Have friends or family members read the questions and listen while you answer them.

Create an interview environment - you sit across from your "board" in a chair, with proper posture. Go through all of the steps - shake their hands and introduce yourself, wait until you are asked to sit down before doing so, etc.

Tim's Tip – Practice reciting your answers in front of a mirror. This allows you to observe your posture, analyze your tone and body language. Trust me, this works!

This is how you prepare for an adversarial interview process – practice!

What happens when you get a question that is not on the provided list?

No problem! The questions are going to have a certain theme (as discussed earlier). Knowing the question concepts and having rehearsed your delivery, you will be ready and confident.

NOTE – Do not curse during your interview. It makes you appear unintelligent and it may offend a board member. Keep it professional.

How are you scored?

Every department is different. There is no national standardized system. You will see board members taking notes. They use the notes to evaluate your performance. The notes will be for the bad AND the good. Do not freak out if you see a lot of note taking. Focus on your answers, not on what board members are doing. A board's score sheet may assess you on the following:

- Appearance/Bearing
- Communication Ability
- Judgment
- Attitude
- Confidence
- Interpersonal Skills - empathy
- Integrity
- Problem Solving Ability

Once the board has concluded its questions, they may wrap up by offering you the opportunity to ask questions. Do not come in with a laundry list of them. If you are looking for a timetable for the next phase, it is okay to ask. Do not assume that you are going to the next phase - ask it in a hypothetical fashion:

"If I were to be selected, what can I expect to happen next?"

"How many are being hired?"

Once the interview is over, stand up and shake each board member's hand, look them each in the eyes and sincerely thank them for their time.

Remember, stay cool during the interview...think iceman. If you are pushed with verbal aggression, do not push back with aggression. As soon as you furrow your brow or lean forward in your chair, they've got you. The more heightened the interviewer gets, the cooler you should be. Maintain confidence from start to finish. Stay upbeat and optimistic. Remain calm but avoid being monotone, boring or negative.

Creating Confidence

As I have said, MANY TIMES, preparation is the key to confidence and confidence is the key to success. I have given you advice, tips, and links to help you prepare for a Law Enforcement testing process. I have also given you guidance on **how** to prepare for a LE interview (oral board) process. Now, you have to put in the work.

What I want to avoid is for you to think that simply reading this guide is sufficient preparation for the LE hiring process and then blame me when you do not get the job. This manual is not magical. It offers you **structure** for your preparation and requires you to **exert significant effort**. Invest time and energy in your future!

Now, once you've properly prepared and have been invited to an oral board interview, do not sabotage yourself while you are waiting for your turn in the hot seat. Believe it or not, **your posture** while you sit waiting to be called in could be hurting your chances for a successful interview.

Our posture, or stances while sitting and standing, has a physiological effect on our bodies. These effects can impact our confidence levels. How is that you ask? Below is a link to one of my favorite TED Talks. The speaker in this particular one is **Amy Cuddy**. Watch it in its entirety and make sure you practice her simple exercises and incorporate them into your daily life, particularly prior to an important or "high stakes" event, such as your interview.

Link:
How Body Language Shapes Who You Are: https://www.ted.com/talks/amy_cuddy_your_body_language_shapes_who_you_are

Tim's Tip – Public safety jobs are a service to the community. Good LE officers approach their jobs selflessly. A good way to show that you are "selfless" is to volunteer for a charity or non-profit organization, such as a local food pantry, soup kitchen or the Special Olympics. You may be asked **why** you want to be a *fill in the blank*. Many people answer that they want to serve their communities or "give back," yet they have done nothing to illustrate this point. Volunteering will help show that you are willing to help with nothing expected in return. Volunteering can be exceptionally rewarding, and, you just may enjoy it.

Section 7: THE BACKGROUND INVESTIGATION

Congratulations! You have made it to the next phase of your law
enforcement hiring process. If things have gone your way, you will
be moving on in the process. What the next phase is will be
different depending on the department. Some agencies may zip you
right into a background investigation. Or, you may have to go
through an assessment center (more on that later). Some agencies
will have you meet with the Chief and/or administrative staff.

If you are invited to meet with the Chief or an administrator, here
are some things to keep in mind:

- The same rules for your attire applies
- Be prompt (that means early)
- No cologne or perfume
- Don't bring items with you (unless told to do so)
- Invoke the Amy Cuddy method while waiting
- Stand up straight and carry yourself with confidence
- Make eye contact and shake hands with everyone in the room
- Introduce yourself while shaking hands
- Wait to be asked to sit down
- Sit straight with your hands in your lap
- Maintain eye contact while speaking with the Chief/Admin
  staff
- Avoid being monotone...be bright with controlled energy
- Answer questions honestly and openly
- When you are done, make sure you shake hands with
  everyone in the room and thank them for their time

Assessment Centers

What are they?

- Assessment Centers will present situational based scenarios.
- You will be put into a scenario with an actor or actors.
- Judges will assess how you handle yourself and how you approach the scenarios.
- Your approach to these scenarios should mimic your approach to scenarios during the oral board. (review that section of this manual)
- Stay calm (remember: "Iceman").
- Maintain command presence (look like a cop, corrections officer, deputy, etc).
- Stay in control (without yelling). If you find yourself yelling, you may have failed.
- Make **fairness** a part of your decision making process.
- When you speak to the actors, look them in the eyes and be CONFIDENT.
- If your scenario deals with quarreling subjects, try to separate them (verbally, not physically).
- Do your best to interview all parties separately.
- Do not take sides. Be impartial and consider both sides of the story
- Remember that you may be asked to solve a problem, even if you do not know the exact law or policy, try to resolve the issue fairly.
- Assessment centers are basically scenario-based questions from the oral board. Approach them as such.

The Background Investigation

If you find yourself in a background investigation, you have succeeded! The background is part of the hiring process. USUALLY, a LE agency will not expend money and resources in a background investigation if they don't intend to hire you.

So, what exactly is a background investigation? This is where a LE agency crawls deep inside your past to make sure you are not a criminal, psychologically imbalanced, undependable, or possess other traits that could potentially place the agency in a bad position. The agency needs to know that you are credible, reliable, stable and that something from your past is not going to come back and cause problems.

How the process starts:

If an agency wishes to hire you, you "should" be given a CONDITIONAL OFFER OF EMPLOYMENT. This means that they will employ you provided you pass their conditions, meaning that your background investigation is acceptable. Some agencies may not provide a formal offer, but you will still need to go through the background.

What to expect in a background investigation:

- LOTS OF PAPERWORK to complete
- Multiple appointments. BE ON TIME FOR ALL APPOINTMENTS!
- You will be asked to sign an information release form
- You will have to fill out a Personal Data Questionnaire (PDQ)

- You will need to obtain a copy of your credit report
- You may be required to obtain an official copy of your high school and/or college transcripts
- Psychological Exams
- Polygraph Exams
- Investigators will conduct interviews with your past and present coworkers, family, friends, neighbors, ex-spouses or significant others; essentially anybody they can reach
- They will call your references and then ask those individuals for references
- Assume they will look at your social media sites (Facebook, Twitter, Instagram, etc, etc.)

Note: If you have bad credit and you still wish to be a law enforcement officer, you need to initiate steps to move your credit in a positive direction. I have seen good candidates washed out of the process due to their terrible credit. If you cannot be responsible enough to pay your bills, then how can you be trusted with a gun and the ability to take a person's freedom?

Another Note: I have also seen candidates washed out of the background process because they were late to background appointments. The officers performing your background are very busy people. They will not take kindly to you being late for an appointment. Also, timeliness speaks to your character and reliability. DON'T BE LATE!

Polygraph Exam

Many agencies require a polygraph exam. I am not a trained polygraphist, nor do I play one on TV. I have worked with many and I know how the process works.

Step 1

Your background investigator will complete a pre-polygraph interview with you. Expect it to last two or more hours. You will be asked many, many personal questions, including questions about your sex life. Trust me, as a former background investigator, these questions are personal and many can be uncomfortable. Just know that background investigations are **confidential**.

Tim's Tips for the Pre-Polygraph Interview:

- DO NOT LIE!!
- DO NOT HOLD ANYTHING BACK!!
- No matter how embarrassed you are, answer the questions thoroughly.
- It has been my experience that most people fail the polygraph based on what they DO NOT say, rather than what they DO say.
- The polygraph process will stress you out - it is supposed to.
- Just relax as much as possible, be open and remember that the interview is confidential.
- **<u>DO NOT LIE!!</u>**

Tim's Note: You MUST be honest during the pre-polygraph interview. You may disclose information about your past that disqualifies you. We cannot undo the past. What is done is done.

It is far better for you to disclose the information than not disclose it and then fail your actual polygraph. Here is an example. Let's say that you disclose that you smoked marijuana within the last nine months. The agency may say that while it is not the end of the world, they are not comfortable with the time proximity and they choose to disqualify you. Okay, it stinks, but if you wait a year and apply with another, or the same, agency, then when they do a background, they can see that you learned from what happened and you took steps (not smoking again and putting time between the incident and your application) to mitigate the indiscretion.

Now, had you not disclosed the marijuana use and then you failed your polygraph exam, you will never get hired in law enforcement – ever. Failing a polygraph in your past is a career killer.

Step 2

Once you complete your pre-polygraph interview, the background investigator will hand off his notes to the polygraphist. A polygraph exam will be scheduled.

When you meet with the polygraphist, guess what? You get to do the pre-polygraph interview over again! Why? Because the polygraphist is looking for inconsistencies. They want to see if you add or take away from your original interview. In my experience, this is where most people fail the polygraph. They failed to disclose something to the background investigator and now that they are about to get tested, they feel compelled to disclose something. That person just got disqualified! As I said earlier, most polygraph disqualifications are due to what is <u>not</u> disclosed, as opposed to what is disclosed.

If the polygraphist feels that both interviews jive, then you will be hooked up to the magic machine. These devices measure your pulse, your breathing, your galvanic responses, and other things I don't know about. The polygraphist will ask "yes" or "no" questions regarding the answers you gave during your interview.

The polygraphist looks at your response charts and interprets them to make a decision as to your level of deceptiveness.

War Story

My agency has an Explorer Post. There was a young man who was a former Explorer that was trying to become a police officer with my agency. He tried several times to no avail. Finally, he made the cutoffs and passed his oral board. The Chief decided to give him a shot. I was assigned to complete his background investigation.

I knew this young man and I liked him. When I met with him he was excited and anxious to be a police officer. He had just obtained his bachelor's degree in criminal justice and was very physically fit.

His first hurdle was with the references he had put on his application. When I called a former boss, he had nothing good to say about the young man. That was a first for me. Usually, references on an application are people that like you (Note: Always **ask** people to be references before you list them).

This did not disqualify him, but it certainly had my interest peaked. During the young man's pre-polygraph interview, he made some disclosures that were concerning, but after a talk with the Chief, it was decided to continue with the background. When the young man had his interview with the polygraph examiner, the disclosures changed – A LOT. What was initially a minor theft turned out to be a burglary – **while** he was a Police Explorer. Needless to say, he was disqualified. It was disappointing for me because I was rooting for the young man.

What's the moral of this story? If you want to work in law enforcement, don't be a friggin' criminal!

Additional Information on Backgrounds

You will be asked to sign a **Release of Information** form.
This is mandatory. The background investigator will need it in
order to conduct interviews and obtain current and past work files.
It is also needed to check your motor vehicle and criminal records
and to check with other law enforcement entities regarding past
contacts. If you do not want to allow it, then you will not continue.

Psychological Exam

You may undergo a psychological/personality test. The test is
lengthy, at least a few hours. You may complete a battery of tests
and may be asked a great deal of questions; oftentimes, the
questions are repeated. This is not a test you can study for. The
questions are not right or wrong. The answers are fed into a
computer and a psychological profile is developed. A trained
psychologist/psychiatrist will evaluate the profile and develop
further questions based on areas of concern. You will then be
interviewed by the person that evaluates your psychological
profile. Based on the results, a level of "risk" is obtained: high,
medium or low. These results will give the hiring agency an idea of
the level of risk that your personality type may bring to the
workplace.

Medical Exam

You may have to undergo a medical exam. This is to determine if
you are physically capable of doing law enforcement work.
You will be screened for drugs (all of them) and you will be poked
and prodded. You may have to do a series of exercises to get your
heart rate up so that it can be measured. Again, this exam is to

screen out any physical issues that may hinder your ability to be a law enforcement officer. Personally, I have never seen anyone disqualified from the physical exam.

Do not worry too much about this part. You are not being screened for the SEAL Teams. The physical is to check for any pre-existing conditions that would prohibit you from working a job that can be stressful and sometimes physically demanding. They are also looking for any conditions that may put you in jeopardy if you are put into a physically demanding situation - such as a heart condition or asthma.

A Quick Disclaimer:

Please understand that there may be issues in your background that could disqualify you from working in law enforcement - even if you are honest with your background investigator. If you have some issues with your background and are not sure if they may be disqualifying, I recommend you call the agency you intend to apply to and ask them.

I would often receive questions during our testing phases. Questions would range from drug use to the department's tattoo policy. You are not going to know the answer unless you ask, right?

PUTTING IT ALL TOGETHER

As I have said many times, there is no short cut to getting yourself thoroughly prepared for the hiring process. What I have illuminated is **the path.** You can now focus your efforts in the right areas to make you the most competitive candidate you can be in the law enforcement job market. If you truly want to work for a LE agency, invest time and energy in yourself and reap the benefits.

I can recall sitting on oral boards for police positions and very occasionally interviewing a candidate that was so impressive, I would speak to my Chief afterwards and recommend that we hire the person before someone else did. That is the candidate that you want to be. **Decide right now** that you are going to dedicate the time and energy into preparation. Decide that YOU WILL BE SUCCESSFUL!

So, let's recap:

- If you have read this manual completely, then you have already decided to put forth the work and that **failure is not an option.**
- Strive to stand out of the crowd in a positive way.
- Ensure you adhere to application deadlines and procedures.
- Always be professional – in your work product, appearance, and attitude.
- Do your homework on your target agency. When you are testing, be familiar with testing locations and requirements, know if you have anything in your past that may prohibit you from being hired.
- Use my techniques to prepare for the PT and the written test. Don't go to the test to simply pass it; go there to **destroy** it.
- Use my techniques to prepare for the oral board interview. Practice, practice, practice!
- If you move on to the background investigation, be professional, be punctual and <u>ALWAYS</u> be truthful!
- The most powerful words in any language are – "I AM...." What comes after those words is what defines you!

I wish you all the best in your pursuit of a career in Law Enforcement. I can tell you from my twenty years of experience that the rewards of working in law enforcement far outweigh the negative aspects – you just have to open your eyes and see them.

Sources:

Schroeder, D. J., Lombardo F.A., (2013) *Barron's Police Officer Exam*, New York, Barron's Educational Series

Rafilson F M, (2008), *Master the Police Officer Exam*, New Jersey, Peterson's Publishing

Foster R. E, Biscontini T. V, (2011), *Police Officer Exam for Dummies*, Massachusetts, Wiley Publishing

Cabane, O. F., *The Science of First Impressions*, https://www.youtube.com/watch?v=_zRZ5j2OO7w

Cuddy, A., *Your Body Language Shapes Who You Are*, https://www.ted.com/talks/ amy_cuddy_your_body_language_shapes_who_you_are

Karp J. R., *3 Interval Training Plans to Build Fitness Fast*, http://www.active.com/running/articles/3-interval-training-plans-to-build-fitness-fast

Ifould, R. (2009). *Acting on Impulse:* https://www.theguardian.com/lifeandstyle/2009/mar/07/first-impressions-snap-decisions-impulse.

44002481R00041

Made in the USA
Middletown, DE
25 May 2017